# Grammar

## Grade 8

Reading and writing are the cornerstones of education. The basics of these skills include reading comprehension and a working knowledge of grammar and spelling. Language class, in which students develop their foundation of English, should be an enjoyable, educational experience for all students. This is possible, however, only if students are conscious of steady progress in their written language, and if they understand what they are doing.

This *Grammar Grade 8* book is part of a *Basics First* series that has been designed to help students succeed in grammar usage. The activities were created to help students feel confident about their grammar skills and help them understand the steps involved in learning these skills.

The pages have been arranged in an easy-to-follow format. This format allows the teacher to choose from a variety of eighth-grade grammar skills that are presented in an interesting, relevant, and age-appropriate manner. Each skill begins with rules and examples. These are followed by intensive practice with interesting information. The skills included are those that every eighth-grade student should possess in order to express himself or herself confidently in spoken and written English.

Today, more emphasis is being placed on the traditional basic subjects. That is because these subjects, including grammar, play a vital role in students' ability to understand the world and to be competent and articulate players in it. Teaching grammar is essential in preparing students to become confident in their English usage.

This book can be used alone or as an integral part of any language program. It can also be used in conjunction with literature-based programs to provide students with the benefits of a well-rounded English language education.

# Sentences—Part I

Name _____

A **sentence** expresses a complete thought. It must contain a subject and a predicate.

The verb connects the subject to the predicate. *Humans have lived on Earth for more than four million years. Humans* is the subject. *Have lived* connects the subject to the predicate, *on Earth for more than four million years.*

There are four types of sentences. A **declarative sentence** makes a statement. *Life was very hard for our ancestors.* An **interrogative sentence** asks a question. *Where did the earliest people live?* An **imperative sentence** commands or requests. *Find out about Neanderthal man by tomorrow.* An **exclamatory sentence** shows excitement, surprise, or other strong feelings. *I see cave paintings!*

## Practice Makes Perfect

Write **declarative, interrogative, imperative**, or **exclamatory** next to each sentence.

1. Early people experienced very few comforts. _____
2. They dwelled in caves or under branches. _____
3. How must they have felt when it rained or snowed? _____
4. Imagine how they felt when they first discovered fire. _____
5. "It's hot!" _____
6. People found out that fire kept them warm, kept away predators, and cooked their meat. _____
7. Could fire be made or did they have to wait for lightning to find it? _____
8. Study the cave paintings to understand the earliest art. _____
9. Those lions are frightened by the fire! _____
10. People spent most of their time looking for food and water. _____
11. They gathered wild grains, fruits, and berries. _____
12. How did they find out that they could eat animals? _____
13. Someone may have found a dead animal and decided to taste it. _____
14. Try some of this bison. _____
15. We can only guess. _____
16. Then they began to kill animals by driving them off cliffs. _____
17. How excited they must have been to invent the first weapon! _____
18. The first weapons might have been rocks that were chipped off until they were sharp. _____
19. Read more about early humans. _____
20. Do you realize that all these changes took place over hundreds of thousands of years? _____
21. The elephants are stampeding! _____
22. That might have been a cry for help. _____
23. During the past century, we have made more advances than in the four million plus years before. _____

FS-30047 Grammar

**Is It or Is It not a Sentence?**     Name _____

Remember that all sentences need both a subject and a predicate. Look at the parts of sentences (or **fragments**) below. They are missing either their subjects or predicates. Determine what is missing in each one. Rewrite the fragments so that they make sense.

1. People didn't. Know their lives were changing.

   _____

2. They could scare off. Many wild animals with fire.

   _____

3. Keeping the fire going. Was a great responsibility.

   _____

4. Soon humans. Learned how to make tools and weapons.

   _____

5. A man. With a stone. Would hit the stone. With a stick.

   _____

6. A piece of stone. Would break. Off it would be sharp.

   _____

7. This sharp tool. Could be used for cutting, slicing, and skinning.

   _____

8. Each member of the tribe. Had a job.

   _____

9. There were. Hunters, gatherers, toolmakers, firekeepers, and cooks.

   _____

10. Just as we do today humans. Have always tried to make their lives better.

   _____

**All About Unnecessary Words**

Words are often added in speech and in writing that don't belong. They are unnecessary because the thought has already been expressed. *Our ancestors they were moving forward. They* isn't necessary because *Our ancestors* is already used as the subject. Therefore, the pronoun *they* as the subject is an unnecessary word. Pronouns are very often used unnecessarily. *My book about early man it makes me glad I live in the present. It* is unnecessary because *My book* is the subject. Other words, such as *see, look, you know,* and *like* are also often used unnecessarily.

**Practice Makes Perfect**

Circle all the unnecessary words in the paragraph below.

Many untruths they have been written about them our ancestors. These tales they have been mainly about cave men dragging women around by the hair using one hand and they holding a club in the other hand. Although women they weren't treated as they are today, they played an important part in the lives of cave people. The women see they would tend the fire, you know make clothing, and cook. Look, the women would like they take care of the kids.

**Try This!**

Pretend you are interviewing a cave person. What would you like to ask him or her? What would you like to tell this ancestor about present-day life?

# Nouns and Pronouns—Part I

Name _____

There are many different types of nouns. A **common noun** names a person, place, or thing. *Dogs are often in the movies. Dog* is a common noun. A **proper noun** names a specific person, place, or thing. *Rin Tin Tin was a dog in the movies. Rin Tin Tin* is a proper noun because it names a specific dog. **Abstract nouns** name something that cannot be heard, seen, touched, tasted, or smelled. *The dog felt fear as the man approached. Fear* is an abstract noun. *Love, hate,* and *happiness* are all abstract nouns. **Concrete nouns** are the opposite of abstract nouns. *Dog* is a concrete noun. You can see, hear, touch, and smell a dog.

Nouns can be singular or plural. A noun that names one person, place, or thing is **singular** (one dog). A noun that names two or more is **plural** (two dogs). Nouns and verbs must agree. *Dogs are smart*, not *Dogs is smart.*

**Collective nouns** name groups of people or things. *A **pride of lions** was in the movie.*

## Practice Makes Perfect

Read the story below about animals in the movies. Underline each common noun. Circle each proper noun.

    Animals have been in the movies since the first movie almost a century ago. Animals, especially dogs and horses, have played both heroes and villains in hundreds of films. Rin Tin Tin was an early canine hero, first appearing in the early to mid 1900s. He was a German shepherd who foiled the bad guys. Lassie first appeared in the movies in the 1950s. "She" was really a "he" but most fans never knew it. Many Lassies have appeared as the clever, loving, and heroic dog. Horses, too, have had their place in the movies. Cowboys such as the Lone Ranger and Roy Rogers had their horses, Silver and Trigger. Silver was a magnificent white horse, and Trigger was a palomino. Some unusual animals that have had movie parts are rats, frogs, dolphins, snakes, bears, wolves, rabbits, and even ferrets. Like human actors, these special animals must be smart, obedient, and willing to take direction.

Circle the abstract nouns in each sentence below. Underline the concrete nouns.

1. Owners show great pride in a well-trained animal actor.

2. Animals must feel great love for their trainers.

3. Animal rights groups are a presence on movie sets.

4. They make certain that animals are treated with respect.

5. Cruelty to animals is not taken lightly.

6. Love for animals makes people want to see them in movies.

Write the correct noun, singular or plural, on the lines.

7. Two or more _____ may play the same role. (dog, dogs)

8. There are special _____ for them. (award, awards)

9. Many _____ are good actors. (animal, animals)

10. In the past, _____ were often hurt on the movie set. (horse, horses)

11. _____ with talented animals can make a good living for themselves and the animals. (Trainer, Trainers)

    FS-30047 Grammar

# Nouns and Pronouns—Part II

Name _____

Write the correct collective noun for each sentence below. If you're stumped on any, look them up in the dictionary. The word list in the box will help you.

1. The _____ of horses pulled the covered wagon.
2. A _____ of lions was rented from the zoo.
3. It was difficult to control the _____ of geese.
4. The dogs wore makeup so that they looked like a _____ of wolves.
5. The _____ of birds was released at just the right time.

| flock |
| --- |
| pack |
| pride |
| gaggle |
| team |

## All About Pronouns

A **subject pronoun** is used as the subject of a sentence. *He was a very friendly dog. He* is used as the subject. An **object pronoun** is used as a direct object. *The dog ate it. Dog* is the subject, and *it* is the direct object. *It* answers the question *what*. An object pronoun can also be used as an **indirect object**. *Show me the dog's pictures. Me* is the indirect object.

An **indefinite pronoun** may refer to a noun. *Everyone wants to see Lassie in action. Everyone* is an indefinite pronoun, as is *anyone, nobody, someone*. A **possessive pronoun** shows ownership. *That dog is **mine**. He is **my** dog.*

Rewrite the sentences below replacing each subject with a pronoun.

6. Lassie starred in many movies and television series.

   _____

7. *Old Yeller* was the sad story of a brave, loyal dog.

   _____

8. Beethoven was a huge St. Bernard.

   _____

9. My friends loved the movie "101 Dalmatians."

   _____

10. Lassie is one of the most famous animal stars ever.

   _____

11. Many animals earn a lot of money.

   _____

Circle the object pronoun in each sentence below.
Write **D** for Direct and **I** for Indirect.

12. He gave me two tickets to the new movie. _____
13. After the movie, we saw them. _____
14. Rin Tin Tin saved him. _____
15. He sent us an article about the animal stars. _____
16. We found them good seats. _____

**Try This!** Write a story about a heroic animal whose story you'd like to see in the movies.

FS-30047 Grammar

# Using Words Correctly—Part I

Name _____

**Take**, **bring**, **learn**, **teach**, **lie**, **lay**, **leave**, **let**, **sit**, and **set** are all words that people may use incorrectly. **Take** means that you are taking something or someone away. It takes the action away from the person who is speaking. *Ancient humans could take fire from place to place.* **Bring** means that the action takes place closer to the person who is speaking. *"Bring the fire to me," the clan's chief said.* The past tense of *take* and *bring* are *took* and *brought*. *Brang* and *brung* are not words in English.

## Practice Makes Perfect

Write the correct word, **take**, **bring**, **took**, or **brought** on the lines below.

1. Hunters would _____ many weapons to the hunt.

2. They would _____ back game to the cave.

3. Women would _____ the game into the cave.

4. "_____ it closer to the light," the old woman said.

5. "We will _____ the fire to the clan over the hill," the chief declared.

6. "We have _____ home food that will last for a week," said the hunter.

**Learn** means to find out about something, to gain knowledge. **Teach** means to instruct, to show another how to gain knowledge or find out about something. **Learn** and **teach** cannot be used interchangeably. Each has its own meaning. It is incorrect to say, *Learn me about early humans.* *Teach me about early humans* is correct. The past tense of each is *learned* and *taught.* (*Teached* is not a word in English.)

Write **teach**, **learn**, **taught**, or **learned** on each line below.

7. Early humans could _____ each other many skills.

8. A mother would _____ her daughter how to cook or make clothing.

9. A son would _____ how to hunt from his father.

10. As humans progressed, they _____ themselves how to plant crops.

11. They _____ that there were many things still to be invented and discovered.

**Lie** and **lay** have very different meanings. Use **lie** to show that someone is reclining: *You can lie on the bed if you have a headache.* But **lay** is used as the past tense of lie. *He lay on the bed reading all day.* (Hint: Don't use *lied* as the past tense of *lie*—it means someone who didn't tell the truth.) It is also used this way. *The hens lay eggs every day.* Remember: You lie in bed, but you lay an egg! The past tense of *lay* is *laid. The hen laid an egg.*

Write **lie, lay,** or **laid** on each line below.

12. Our ancestors didn't have time to _____ around in the cave.

13. If they were sick, they were able to _____ for a short time.

14. They might have seen wild fowl _____ eggs.

15. Fowl _____ eggs and people gathered them.

FS-30047 Grammar

# Using Words Correctly—Part II

Name _____

**Leave** means that one is departing from a place. *It was hard to leave the safe cave.* It also means to allow to stay or to remain. *They had to leave the cave paintings behind.* The past tense of *leave* is *left. They left at the break of day.*

**Let** means to permit, to allow. *They let the next people go into the cave. Let* (not *letted*) is the present and past tense. *They had let people use the cave before.*

Write **leave, left,** or **let** on the lines below.

1. When the people _____, they moved to places where there was more food.

2. They _____ scouts go on ahead and look for game or other food.

3. When they found a suitable place, they _____ to gather food.

4. Do you think they were sad when they had to _____ their homes?

5. What they _____ behind wasn't important compared to the need to find food.

6. How would you feel if you had to _____ your home?

7. Would you _____ your parents know how you felt?

8. What would you want to _____ the least?

9. _____ people alone and they will find a way to live.

10. People have _____ their homes for many reasons over the millennia.

Answer the questions in numbers 6, 7, and 8 above. Use **let, leave,** and **left** at least once.

6. _____

7. _____

8. _____

**Set** means to put something away, down, or aside. *They set the food down and left.* **Set** can also be used in the following ways: *He set the table. The sun set in the west.* It can also mean to start on a journey. *He set out for the wilderness.* **Sat** is the past tense of **sit**: *He sat on the rock.* You can **sit** at the table, **set** the table, **sit** beside the table, and **set** the table down.

Read the story below. Write **set, sit,** or **sat** on the lines.

"_____ down and I'll tell you a story," said my uncle Ned, rumpling my curly hair. "Come and _____ a spell." Uncle Ned's stories tended to go on and on, so I decided to pass. "Sorry, Unk," I said as sadly as I could muster, "Mom asked me to _____ the table. "Okay, but you'll be sorry," he warned. "This story has been in our family since Hector was a pup." He always said that, and I never did find out who Hector was. So I _____ down my books and _____ next to my uncle. He told me a story until the sun _____ . It was about my grandfather and how he _____ out for the Yukon looking for gold in the old days. As I _____ there, I thought, these family stories are worth a lot. I think I'll listen more carefully from now on. Maybe someday I'll _____ them down on paper.

**Try This!** Ask an older person in your family to tell a family story. Write it in detail.

FS-30047 Grammar

# Pronouns and Antecedents—Part I

Name _____

**Pronouns** are very useful for making writing more interesting, but their meanings must be clear. *Donald took his brother to see "Call of the Wild." He thought it was a very exciting movie. His, he,* and *it* are all pronouns. *Someone thought the movie was very exciting.* Was that someone Donald or his brother?

The noun or group of words to which a pronoun refers is called the **antecedent**. The antecedent must clearly refer to the pronoun. In order to ensure this, you may have to repeat a noun or rewrite the sentence for clarity. *Donald took his brother to see "Call of the Wild." His brother thought it was a very exciting movie.* Pronouns must agree with their antecedents.

*The kittens were found by Mr. and Mrs. Jones when they were six weeks old.* Were the kittens or the Joneses six weeks old? The meaning can be made clear by changing the sentence to *The six-week-old kittens were found by Mr. and Mrs. Jones,* or *Mr. and Mrs. Jones found kittens that were six weeks old.* By eliminating the pronoun *they* and rewriting the sentence, it is clear that the kittens were six weeks old. (Hint: Pronouns must also agree in number.)

## Practice Makes Perfect

Rewrite the sentences below so that the antecedent is followed by the pronoun that makes its meaning clear.

1. *Oliver Twist* was written by Charles Dickens. He seemed to be a poor orphan.

   _____

2. *Dombey and Son* by Dickens is a favorite story of my cousin. He wrote it to stress the evils of loving money.

   _____

3. *Little Lord Fauntleroy* was written by Frances Hodgson Burnett. He had a rich old uncle.

   _____

4. Lucy Boston wrote stories about the children of Green Knowe. They were ghostly.

   _____

5. Heidi is a girl who lives with her grandfather and some goats in the Swiss Alps. They find each other strange at first.

   _____

6. Stories about Harriet the Spy and her friends are much appreciated by the kids in our class. They enjoy adventures.

   _____

7. *The Great Brain* books were written by John Fitzgerald for boys and girls. They are really fun.

   _____

8. Anastasia Krupnik is a heroine created by Lois Lowry. She is smart, brave, and funny.

   _____

# Pronouns and Antecedents—Part II

Name _____

Underline the correct antecedent for each pronoun below. Write the correct pronoun on each line. Make certain that the pronoun and antecedent agree in number and gender.

1. His favorite characters are the boys from *Lord of the Flies*. _____ held lots of meetings.

2. *Treasure Island* is about a boy named Jim Hawkins who gets mixed-up with pirates. _____ searches for real pirate treasure.

3. *The Hardy Boys* is a series of adventure books. _____ is about two brothers.

4. *Tom Sawyer* is a great book. _____ was a mischievous lad.

5. *The Little Prince* is a small book written by Antoine St.-Exupéry. _____ wrote it in French, but it has been translated into many languages.

6. One of Mark Twain's best works is *Huckleberry Finn.* _____ was a boy who lived on the Mississippi River.

7. *Little Women* was about four sisters, Jo, Amy, Beth, and Meg. _____ shared many hardships.

8. A book that has been a favorite for many years is *Anne of Green Gables*. _____ is about a spunky, smart orphan.

9. *The Adventures of the Bobbsey Twins* were popular long ago. _____ are not read as much anymore.

10. If you're interested in really old tales, check out *Aladdin* or *Ali Baba and the Forty Thieves*. _____ are great stories!

Underline the antecedents in the following story. Circle the pronouns.

Tall tales are funny, memorable stories. They are about heroes and their usually hard-to-believe feats of strength and bravery. One favorite hero of American folk tales is Paul Bunyan. He had a huge blue ox named Babe. It helped him with his brave acts.

Paul Bunyan was a lumberjack. He could, of course, fell the tallest, thickest tress there were in the forest. Paul could stop raging rivers and knock down mountains. He was a great example for people who work outdoors.

Pecos Bill is another legendary hero. He performed feats out west and was an inspiration for cowboys, or so it is said. Other heroes of tall tales are Mike Fink, who was a riverboat captain, and John Henry, a railroad worker who died on the job. Some folk heroes, like John Chapman, really did exist. He was also known as Johnny Appleseed. He planted apples all over the countryside. The tall tale part is that he supposedly planted seeds just about all over the country, which is not really true or possible. Tall tales are an interesting part of a nation's history.

**Try This!**

On the back of this page, make up a tall tale about a hero you invent and his or her remarkable feats. Circle the antecedents and underline the pronouns.

FS-30047 Grammar

# Action Verbs

**Action verbs** name actions. These verbs may consist of a verb and a helping verb. An action verb expresses action and tells what the subject does. *Ancient Egyptians may have invented farming. Ancient Egyptians* is the subject. The action verb is *invented.*

Action verbs show either mental or physical action. *Run, hide, race,* and *talk* are all **physical actions.** *The farmers raced against time because the Nile would soon overflow. Think, wonder, learn,* and *agree* are all **mental actions.** *Historians agree that the Egyptians were talented, clever people.*

## Practice Makes Perfect

Read the sentences below about ancient farmers. Circle all the action verbs.

1. People farmed when they learned how to plant seeds.

2. They also discovered how to domesticate previously wild animals.

3. The invention of the wheel about 5,000 years ago created new work for farmers.

4. Early farmers plowed their fields by hand.

5. Many farmers in ancient Egypt helped build the pyramids during their off seasons.

6. They worked hard to build the pharaohs' tombs.

7. The Nile Valley and the Nile Delta rank among the world's best farming areas.

8. The Nile overflowed its banks every year at approximately the same time.

9. The farmers of Egypt waited for this natural irrigation to water their crops.

10. They dug irrigation channels to direct the water to their thirsty plants.

11. Farmers paid taxes with crops such as grain.

12. They bartered for the necessities of life with their crops.

13. In times of drought, they might sell themselves into servitude to help their families.

14. The Egyptians depended upon the Nile for many things.

15. In those days long ago, the crocodile and the hippo shared the waters of the river.

Look at the underlined action verbs below. Decide whether they are **mental** or **physical** and write **M** or **P** on the lines.

16. The world's earliest civilization <u>developed</u> in Mesopotamia. ____

17. Egyptian civilization <u>began</u> in about 3100 B.C. ____

18. When King Menes <u>united</u> Egypt, that area prospered. ____

19. Soon, the Egyptians <u>built</u> pyramids. ____

20. They <u>conquered</u> their neighbors. ____

21. Egyptians <u>thought</u> their kingdom would last forever. ____

22. Their way of life was <u>imitated</u> by neighboring kingdoms such as Kush. ____

23. By the time Cleopatra <u>died</u>, there was nothing left of the glory of Egypt. ____

24. You can <u>memorize</u> the time line of Egypt to help understand its history. ____

 FS-30047 Grammar

# Linking, Transitive, and Intransitive Verbs

Name _____

**Linking verbs** are followed by words that explain or identify the subject of a sentence. They are found in the predicate of the sentence. These words may be nouns or adjectives. If the word following the linking verb is a noun, it is called a **predicate noun**. *Many ancient Egyptians were farmers. Were* is the linking verb. *Farmers* is the predicate noun. A **predicate adjective** is an adjective that follows a linking verb. *The weather in Egypt was hot. Hot* describes the weather in Egypt, so it is a predicate adjective. Linking verbs include forms of **be** and verbs of the senses. *Seem, appear, taste, smell, look, hear,* and *become* can all be used as linking verbs.

## Practice Makes Perfect

Read each sentence below. Underline each linking verb. On the lines, write **N** if it is followed by a predicate noun and **A** if it is followed by a predicate adjective.

1. We think Mesopotamia was the cradle of civilization. _____

2. The population of Mesopotamia grew large. _____

3. The climate was dry and hot. _____

4. There are two rivers in Mesopotamia _____

5. Water for crops was available along the rivers. _____

6. The people were happy. _____

7. The Sumerians were industrious and built the world's first cities. _____

8. This group of people is famous for developing the first civilization. _____

9. The Sumerians were also great inventors. _____

10. They were smart enough to invent a system of writing called *cuneiform*. _____

11. Wedge-shaped characters and word pictures were part of this writing system. _____

12. Sumerians were a very advanced people. _____

13. Many historians believe that the Sumerians were ahead of the people of their time. _____

14. Like many mighty empires before and after, Sumer is an important part of history. _____

A **transitive verb** needs a direct object. It is an action verb. *Pharaohs built the tombs. Built* is the transitive verb. Its direct object is the noun *tombs.* An **intransitive verb** can stand alone. *The lion roared* is intransitive. There is no direct object after the action verb *roared.*

Underline each transitive verb in the sentences below. Circle the direct object of each transitive verb. Draw a rectangle around each intransitive verb.

15. The banks flooded.

16. The water flooded the fields.

17. The people fought the rising water.

18. The armies fought.

**Try This!** Write a letter to a friend telling him or her about the wonderful things that exist in your world. What are the greatest inventions our civilization has produced?

FS-30047 Grammar

Name _____

Tenses affect the way people write and speak. They affect the sequence of events, or the order in which things happen. *He invents something valuable* is in the **present tense**. *He invented something valuable* is in the **past tense**. The past tense of many verbs is formed by adding **-ed** to the present tense: *invent, invented*. There are, however, many irregular verbs in English that do not follow the rule. The **future tense** of verbs is formed by adding the helping verbs *shall* or *will* before the verb: *I shall invent a better mousetrap. He will invent a fuel-efficient car someday.*

## Practice Makes Perfect

Rewrite the sentences below so that the verbs are in the correct tenses.

1. Thomas Edison will invent the light bulb.

   _____

2. Da Vinci thinks man can fly.

   _____

3. Someone invented a ship that took us to Mars.

   _____

4. The computer will revolutionize the business world.

   _____

5. Many inventions will change the world in the nineteenth century.

   _____

6. Orville and Wilbur Wright work on an invention called the airplane.

   _____

7. Samuel Morse will have a code that he will invent named after him.

   _____

8. The wheel will be the greatest invention the world will know.

   _____

9. Television will be seen by hundreds of millions of people.

   _____

10. Simple inventions such as gloves and zippers change the world, too.

   _____

Cross out the incorrect tenses in the paragraph below and write the correct ones above them.

Human beings will be marvelous creatures. We will invent more things in the nineteenth and twentieth centuries than in our entire five-million-year history. We invent things that we only imagined now—cars that flew above the highways, computers that fit on a watch, airships that zoomed across the oceans in minutes. The ability to invent is what made humans the highest form of life on Earth.

# Tenses—Part II

Name _____

The **present perfect tense** is formed by the helping verb **has** or **have** and the past participle of a verb. It names an action that is not completely over, but is closely associated with the present. *Humans have invented things for many years.* Notice that *many years* is not a definite time. The helping verb *have* is followed by the past participle *invented.* This tense can also name an action that began in the past and is still going on in the present. *We have attended school for a long time.* This indicates that we have attended school, and we are still doing so.

## Practice Makes Perfect

Write the present perfect tense of each verb in parentheses.

1. Skyscrapers _____ for most of this century. (exist)

2. People _____ at skyscrapers and _____ them. (marvel, visit)

3. Millions of people _____ the Empire State Building, the Sears Tower, and the World Trade Center. (see)

4. These buildings are so tall that visitors _____ lightning and rain below them while they are bathed in sunshine. (experience)

5. These buildings _____ during heavy winds. (sway)

6. Skyscrapers _____ tourists and natives alike since they were built. (intrigue)

7. The Empire State Building _____ as many as 20 bolts of lightning during a storm. (absorb)

8. This building _____ as many as 10,000 tenants as an office building. (house)

9. When heavy winds _____ it to sway, it _____. (cause, creak)

10. Skyscrapers _____ people in many cities throughout the world. (thrill)

The **past perfect tense** is formed by the helping verb **had** and the past participle of the verb. It names an action that happened before another action or event in the past. *We had finished our experiment before dinner. Had finished* is the past perfect tense and *dinner* is the other event.

Write the past perfect tense in each sentence below using the verb in parentheses.

11. Our teacher _____ us to invent something useful. (challenge)

12. I _____ about it all night without coming up with one idea. (think)

13. It was time for school, and I _____ for my friend Trisha for 10 minutes. (wait)

14. I saw her coming, and she said she _____ all the way. (run)

15. What _____ to her, I wondered. (happen)

16. She _____ her invention late last night and wanted to tell me about it. (see)

17. What _____ her up all night? (keep)

18. It _____ in a dream, she told me breathlessly. (come)

**Try This!** Finish the story above. What is this great invention? Does it work? Does she get rich? How about her friend (who can be you in the story)?

# Run-on and Compound Sentences—Part I

Name _____

As you know, sentences must have a subject (what the sentence is about) and a predicate (what happens to the subject). If they have more than one of these parts and have thoughts that run together without punctuation, they are called **run-on sentences**. Run-ons are frequently bound together with words such as *and, but, then,* and *because. We studied about the different classes of animals and it was interesting and I learned a lot but the most interesting fact was that there are so many different kinds of mammals and we all look different* and so on. Run-on sentences ruin good ideas, stories, and term papers you write. Look at the run-on sentence above and notice how it looks when it's corrected: *We studied about the different classes of animals. It was interesting and I learned a lot. The most interesting fact was that there are so many different kinds of mammals. We all look different.* This is just one way to correct the run-on sentence above.

## Practice Makes Perfect

Rewrite the run-on below so that the story makes sense. Remove words if necessary.

What do the star-nosed mole, people, and the gigantic blue whale have in common and if you said they are all mammals you are right and they all breathe air through their lungs and nurse their young and they have a more well-developed brain and hair but if you said they all also maintain a constant body temperature, you are right and all mammals except for a few for example the echidna and platypus and both of them are from Australia are born live but they lay eggs and there are about 4,000 kinds of mammals on Earth.

_____
_____
_____
_____
_____
_____
_____
_____

A **compound sentence** contains two or more sentences connected by **and, or,** or **but.** A compound sentence also contains two or more subjects and predicates. **And, or,** and **but** are called **conjunctions.** Each conjunction has a specific meaning. **And** means *in addition to.* **But** means *except for this* or *on the contrary.* **Or** means *another possibility exists. Rabbits are very furry,* **and** *ferrets are hairy, too. Let's go to the museum* **or** *we'll miss the prehistoric animals exhibit. Mammals are numerous,* **but** *insects are much more numerous.* Notice that a comma sometimes separates the two parts of the sentence.

# Run-on and Compound Sentences—Part II

Name _____

Don't confuse a compound sentence with a sentence that has a compound subject or a compound predicate. In a sentence with a compound subject, there is only one subject part. A sentence that has a compound predicate has only one predicate part. Compound sentences, however, are made of simple sentences joined together by conjunctions. Each part can stand independently of the other.

## Practice Makes Perfect

Read each sentence below. If it is a compound sentence, write **CS** on the line. If it is a simple sentence, write **SS** on the line.

1. Mammals depend on their bodies to maintain temperature, but reptiles and amphibians depend on their environment. _____

2. Without other mammals, humans would probably be long extinct, and the world might be taken over by insects. _____

3. There are about 20,000 species of fishes and more than 800,000 varieties of insects on our planet. _____

4. A most unusual mammal is the Tasmanian devil, and he is every bit as fierce as the cartoons show him to be. _____

5. The devil lives on the island of Tasmania and eats small mammals and reptiles. _____

6. The star-nosed mole is a mammal found in North America. _____

7. This mole has fleshy feelers in the shape of a star on its nose, and the mole is an expert swimmer and diver. _____

8. The male proboscis monkey of the rain forest has a huge nose, but this doesn't stop him from being attractive to female monkeys. _____

9. Wart hogs have large curved tusks, and they have three large "warts" between their eyes and their tusks. _____

10. The world of mammals is varied, but long-extinct mammals would make it even more interesting if they existed today. _____

Change the simple sentences below into compound sentences.

11. The sloth seems lazy and weak. It has powerful claws for defense.

    _____

12. The sloth must stay in trees for long periods. It can be easy prey on the ground.

    _____

13. Sloths eat leaves, buds, and young twigs. They sleep during the day.

    _____

**Try This!** What mammal would you nominate as the world's most weird? In a paragraph, tell why. Use at least one compound sentence.

# Adverbs and Intensifiers—Part I

Name _____

**Adverbs** tell more about verbs. They answer the questions *how, when, where, how much,* and *how often*. In the sentence In the sentence *Move quickly so we're not locked in at the library, quickly* answers *how* or *in what manner. Once in the library, we go everywhere. Everywhere* is the adverb that answers the question *where. We frequently visit the library. Frequently* answers *how often.* Adverbs can describe adjectives, action verbs, or even other adverbs. *We tiptoed around the library particularly quietly.* Both adverbs answer the question *how.*

Many adverbs are formed by adding the suffix **-ly** to an adjective. *It was a clear night. It was* **certainly** *a clear night.* Many other adverbs do not end in **-ly.** They answer *when, where,* and *how.* Look at the list below to learn some of these adverbs.

| **When** | **Where** | **How** |
|---|---|---|
| soon, later, afterwards, once, before, first, often, sometimes | here, there, away, far, together, everywhere, anywhere, nowhere | hard, fast, long, quick, alike, slow, well |

## Practice Makes Perfect

Read the story below. Circle all the adverbs you find.

Most kids think seriously at one time or another about running away from home. I'm not different, really. I had this humongously gross fight with my sister, and my mother and father took her side. I quietly went to my room, got my backpack, and slipped away just to get out for awhile. Dejectedly, I went to the wonderfully quiet library. Our library is beautifully decorated with gargoyles, lions, and all that old-time library stuff. It's cavernously large, and you can lose yourself there quickly. It would be the place my sister would look for me last. She loudly proclaims her dislike for reading whenever she can.

I could hide safely in the library, I knew. Well, I'd like to tell you that it closed, and I hid so well that nobody ever found me. That's not what really happened. The guards grouchily told me to leave. I heard them laughingly tell people, "They usually don't hide in the library." To make it worse, I had to pay all my overdue library fines. Running away is hardly worth the trouble. Next time, I'll obnoxiously suggest that my sister run away.

Circle the adverbs in each sentence below. Write **how, when, where, how much,** or **how often** to show how each adverb is used. Some sentences may contain more than one adverb.

1. It would be fun to have a gnarly adventure in the library sometimes. _____ _____

2. Maybe the Egyptian mummies from a book would scarily come to life. _____ _____

3. If they did, I would be a hero and hit them hard on the head. _____

4. Perhaps my favorite mystery heroes would easily come out of the books. _____ _____

5. We could go on a dangerously great adventure together. _____ _____

6. Maybe I could finally have some fun that is slightly not boring. _____ _____ _____

7. Later, I would tell everyone about it. _____

8. I suppose hardly anybody would ever believe me. _____ _____

9. But I'll try anything once. _____

10. I would definitely become famous if I could prove it. _____

# Adverbs and Intensifiers—Part II

Name _____

**Intensifiers** are words that show to what extent a trait or characteristic is present in an adjective or an adverb. *She is an exceptionally fluent reader. Exceptionally* shows how fluent she is. *Fluent* is the adjective that describes *reader.* Following is a list of common intensifiers: *too, somewhat, partly, completely, hardly, scarcely, barely, wholly, slightly, unusually, really, surely, mostly, very, exceptionally, so, quite.* Intensifiers are another way to obtain more information about an adjective or adverb.

## Practice Makes Perfect

Circle the intensifier in each sentence below. Write **adverb** or **adjective** on the line to tell which the intensifier describes.

1. You can find a lot more besides highly interesting books in the library. _____

2. Today's libraries have something for almost every person. _____

3. You can be satisfied with a selection of totally great CDs. _____

4. If you really truly love movies, there's a great variety at the library. _____

5. Computers are almost always available. _____

6. If you take research quite seriously, there is a well-stocked reference desk. _____

7. Libraries terribly often have rooms for musical and dramatic performances. _____

8. Librarians are completely helpful for whatever your needs may be. _____

9. Your local library may also have a totally computerized card catalog. _____

10. Explore your excitingly modern library to thoroughly enjoy it. _____

## Comparing With Adverbs

Adverbs show comparison. The **comparative form of adverbs** compares two actions. It usually adds **-er** or **more** to show the comparison. *The closing bell in the library rang louder than usual. The closing bell in the library rang more loudly than usual* is also correct. The **superlative form** of adverbs compares more than two actions. *It is the loudest bell of all the libraries in town.* The word *most* can also be used as a superlative. *That guard is the most friendly of them all at the library. Most* is most often used for adverbs that do not have comparative or superlative forms. *Less* and *least* are also used before adverbs. *She is the least capable of the volunteers in the library. We are less certain of her talents than previously.* (Hint: When using **-er** or **-est,** do not also use **more, most, less,** or **least.**)

Write comparative or superlative words in the sentences below. Read the whole sentence to get the hints to help you write the correct word.

11. I read _____ often than you and have read four books just this week.

12. She speaks _____ clearly and is hard to understand.

13. That is the _____ book I have ever read, and it really made me laugh.

14. He plays the guitar in the library _____ than any other performer.

**Try This!** Write about your library experiences—how often you go, what types of books you check out, what other services you use, whether or not you think libraries are necessary in communities, etc.

# Adjectives—Part I

Name _____

**Adjectives** modify nouns and pronouns. They tell **what kind, how many,** or **which one**.

Adjectives describe shape, size, color, feeling, and condition. *English is a complex language. Complex* describes the noun *language.* It answers what kind. *Many people all over the world speak English. Many* answers the question *how many. This language is spoken by more than one in every eight people. This* answers the question *which one.*

## Practice Makes Perfect

Read the facts below about English. Write one of the adjectives from the box below on each line.

1. English is used in almost _____ part of the world.

2. The _____ language is used by more people than English.

3. English is a combination of Latin, German, Italian, Spanish, and other _____ languages.

4. English spread throughout the world as a result of various _____ events.

5. It is almost a _____ language in countries such as India, Pakistan, and Bangladesh.

6. English contains more _____ words than words of any other language.

7. Scandinavians gave us _____ words, many beginning with *sk-* or *sc-* (i.e. sky, skin, scare).

8. They are also responsible for _____ words such as *they, them,* and *their.*

9. There are about a half a billion _____ speakers in the world.

10. _____ English words (those that have always been part of the language) include *woman, man, sun, hand, love, go,* and *eat.*

11. English has a _____ vocabulary than any other language.

12. It has an _____ 600,000-word vocabulary.

13. One of the marks of an _____ person is an _____ vocabulary.

14. We borrowed _____ words such as *wigwam* and *tomahawk* from Native Americans.

15. A number of words are formed by combining two words and are called _____ words.

16. The _____ Roman legions conquered the Celts, followed by the fierce Germanic tribes—the Angles (that's where the name England comes from), the Saxons, and the Jutes.

17. Latin and German became a _____ part of our language.

| | | | | | |
|---|---|---|---|---|---|
| useful | colorful | educated | larger | English | astonishing |
| Chinese | foreign | second | historical | German | common | Native |
| compound | every | permanent | mighty | extensive | |

# Adjectives—Part II

Name _____

## Demonstrative Adjectives

**Demonstrative adjectives** are used to modify a word, phrase, or clause used as a noun. These commonly used adjectives are **this, that, these,** and **those.** It is important to remember that the demonstrative adjective must agree in number with the noun—**this** and **that** are singular while **these** and **those** are plural. Each one stands alone and is incorrect if used with **here** or **there.** (*This here cat* or *That there dog.*) *This language is not hard to learn. This* indicates closeness, something near. *That language is very hard to learn. That* indicates something farther away. *Them* is not a demonstrative adjective. *Them languages is taught in high school* is incorrect. *Those* or *These languages are taught in high school* is correct.

## Practice Makes Perfect

Choose the correct demonstrative adjective for each sentence. Cross out any unnecessary words.

1. _____ here book on English origins is right in front of me.

2. I found _____ there book in the library.

3. _____ language of ours is more difficult for Asians to learn than for South Americans.

4. That's because _____ here Asian languages haven't the Latin words that are familiar to Spanish and Portuguese speakers.

5. _____ here languages (French, Italian, and Spanish) are not too hard for us to learn.

6. I spoke English to _____ Russians I met yesterday, and it was very frustrating all around.

7. _____ people from Russia even have a different alphabet. It's called the Cyrillic alphabet.

8. Do you remember the name of _____ language that was supposed to become an international language for all humankind?

9. _____ other languages are widely used, but _____ here one was called Esperanto.

10. _____ there would be amazing to have one language for all the world!

## Adjectives That Compare

Like adverbs, some adjectives add **-er** or **-est** to form the comparative and superlative. *Chinese is older than English.* Adding **-er** to *old* makes a comparison between two things. *English is not the oldest language in the world.* Adding **-est** to *old* makes a comparison with more than two things. Some common comparative and superlative adjectives are **good, better, best, well, better, bad, worse,** and **worst.**

Write the correct adjective in each sentence below.

11. Which is _____ to learn, English or Spanish? (easy)

12. The _____ of the two students in French is the _____ one. (good, young)

13. French pronunciation is _____ than German for many people. (hard)

14. Most people think their native language is _____ than any other. (good)

**Try This!** Learn Pig Latin! Just take the initial consonant off any word, add it to the end with **-ay** tagged on. So *good luck* becomes *ood-gay uck-lay*! How about words that begin with vowels? *Easy*! That's *easy-ay*!

# Participles—Part I

Name _____

A **participle** modifies a noun or a pronoun. Participles have **-ing** or **-ed** endings with helping verbs, if necessary, depending upon how they are used. Don't forget that irregular verbs have irregular past participles. *Stricken by environmental pollution, Earth is always trying to rebound. Stricken* and *trying* are the participles in this sentence.

## Practice Makes Perfect

Read the story below about the environment. Circle every participle you find.

People have been dirtying the air, land, and water of Earth for millions of years. Archaeologists have proven that from the beginning of human life on this lovely planet, we have been polluting it. Early man, of course, was throwing out small-time garbage compared to people today. Littering a cave or two, leaving bones around, and drawing on cave walls are not the same as the major polluting we see being done today. Gas, smoke, chemicals, pesticides, garbage that's not biodegradable, and chlorofluorocarbons are poisoning our planet. Not being able to discard this planet and go on to another, we'd better fix it. To stop, though, we might have to stop using many conveniences that we now enjoy. Reducing pollution in some urban areas has made a difference. Recycling garbage has also helped. Most of today's pollution is resulting from burning gasoline and coal. Oil spilling from freighters has been responsible for the deaths of ocean life and shore life. Let's give our planet a break, Earthlings! It's going to be our home for a long, long time!

On each line below, write the noun or pronoun to which each underlined participle is connected, to which it refers.

1. Most pollution is caused by <u>burning</u> garbage and trash. _____ _____

2. People <u>living</u> on Earth need to stop <u>polluting</u> it. _____ _____

3. Until the 1700s and 1800s, people were not <u>polluting</u> Earth very much. _____

4. By governments <u>enforcing</u> laws, much pollution can be <u>decreased</u>. _____ _____

5. Governmental representatives need to be <u>persuaded</u> to enforce the laws. _____

6. People <u>moving</u> to the cities from rural areas has greatly increased pollution. _____

7. By <u>reducing</u>, <u>recycling</u>, and <u>reusing</u>, we can all help stop pollution. _____

8. Gas-guzzling cars must be <u>given</u> up someday. _____

9. Electric cars have been <u>invented</u> but are not practical. _____

10. Sewage <u>contains</u> large amounts of pollutants from plant and animal matter. _____

11. Smog is <u>causing</u> illness in millions of people. _____

12. Smog has even <u>caused</u> some monuments to pit and begin to wear away. _____

13. Have we <u>forgotten</u> how to take care of Earth? _____

14. <u>Left</u> alone, our planet will turn into a massive garbage dump. _____

15. It's is a big job, but we humans are capable of <u>cleaning</u> Earth! _____

# Participles—Part II

Name _____

A **participial phrase** includes a participle and other words, including the word that the participle modifies. The participial phrase must be as close to the word it modifies as possible or it will lose its meaning. *Seeing the pollution, the smog was all over the city. Seeing the pollution* is a dangling participial phrase. It just kind of hangs in mid-air, and the way it is read, it seems that the smog was seeing the pollution. It can be changed to *Seeing the pollution, we were disgusted that the smog was all over the city. While waiting for the trash collector, I lined the trash cans up at the curb.* The participial phrase modifies *I. I was waiting for the trash collector, and I lined the trash cans up at the curb.*

## Practice Makes Perfect

Rewrite each sentence below so that there are no dangling participles.

1. By treating sewage plants, the water becomes cleaner.
   _____

2. Settling in the lungs, we can get asthma or other illnesses from smog.
   _____

3. Failing to save Earth, the planet will be unlivable.
   _____

4. Recycling cans, bottles, and newspapers, Earth will be cleaner.
   _____

5. Driving cars that use lots of gas, pollution will only get worse.
   _____

6. Collecting recyclables for money, containers can be used for each pickup.
   _____

7. Earning money for a field trip, the school sent us to science camp.
   _____

8. Finding garbage in the street, it was picked up and thrown in the proper place.
   _____

9. Realizing the danger of pollution, the article in the paper was read by all.
   _____

10. Being a person who cares about the environment, the newspaper carried my article.
    _____

Finish the sentences below so that there are no dangling participial phrases.

11. Seeing the truck belching smoke, _____

12. Taking my recyclables to the recycling center, _____

13. Writing about pollution, _____

14. Doing the laundry, _____

15. Encouraged by everyone's efforts,_____

**Try This!** Find out what your city or town does to stop pollution. Write a paragraph or two explaining it. Then write a letter to your local newspaper giving ideas on how to make the world a cleaner place in which to live!

# Gerunds—Part I

A **gerund** is the present participial form of a verb ending in **-ing.** It is used like a noun. Sometimes a gerund is used as the **simple subject** of a sentence. *Exploring is not for the timid or the meek. Exploring* is the simple subject. It is also a noun. Participles are also used as the **main verb in a verb phrase**. *Scientists are discovering that many people "found" America before Columbus.* The participle *discovering* is the main verb in the verb phrase *are discovering.*

A participle used as a gerund may also appear as the **direct object of a verb**. The object of a verb receives the action of a verb and answers the question **what**. *The Vikings enjoyed exploring. Exploring* is a noun and is used as the direct object of the verb *enjoyed* and answers the question **what**. A verb form ending in **-ing** is also used as an adjective. *The exploring Vikings were adventurers. Exploring* describes Vikings and is used as an adjective. So remember, a present participle can be used as a verb phrase, as an adjective describing a noun or a pronoun, and as a gerund used as a noun or as a simple subject.

## Practice Makes Perfect

Underline the gerund in each sentence below. Write **SS** if the gerund is the simple subject and **DO** if it is the direct object of the verb.

1. Leading is something Eric the Red excelled at. _____

2. Eric was greatly affected by the outlawing of his father. _____

3. Eric and his father began planning to move to Iceland. _____

4. Being exiled for three years from Iceland was tough for Eric. _____

5. Being declared an outlaw made Eric sail from Iceland into the unknown sea. _____

6. His three-year sentence as an outlaw kept him exploring. _____

7. Adventuring led him to a new land he named Greenland. _____

8. But Greenland was a place that was forbidding. _____

9. Eric and his men settled on Greenland farming and raising sheep. _____ _____

10. Eric thought falling from a horse was bad luck. _____

11. Exploring was in the blood of Leif Ericson, son of Eric the Red. _____

12. Telling stories about Leif Ericson was important to Norse people. _____

13. Ericson was born in Iceland, and it was growing up there that made him conscious of his father's place in Norse society. _____

14. Sailing was a skill Ericson learned from his father. _____

15. He was seeking a land that had been sighted by a Norse sea captain. _____

# Gerunds—Part II

Name _____

In the sentences below, write whether the *ing* participles are used as the main verb in a **verb phrase**, as an **adjective**, or as a **gerund**. Underline each participle.

1. Vikings began exploring. _____
2. Leif Ericson was preaching Christianity to the pagan Norsemen. _____
3. He was sailing farther south when he discovered forest land. _____
4. He took his sailing ship to a place where grapes were growing. _____ _____
5. As the men were making wine from the grapes, they decided to name the place Vinland. _____
6. Some historians are still thinking that the "grapes" may have really been cranberries or gooseberries. _____
7. The men began building. _____
8. Their logging skills helped them cut timber to take back to Greenland where there were few trees. _____
9. Building a shed for their ship to protect it was a good idea. _____
10. Ericson and his crew rescued victims of a shipwreck while returning to Greenland. _____
11. The drowning men were taken on board. _____
12. The grateful survivors insisted on giving Ericson and his crew their cargo. _____
13. Discovering exactly where Ericson landed is difficult. _____
14. Sailing is mysterious when you discover new places. _____
15. Eric the Red must have been happy that he was living to see his son's glory. _____
16. Eric's death made the returning Vikings sad. _____
17. Ericson's brother, Thorwald, was continuing the legacy of exploration. _____
18. He was killed by attacking Indians on one of his trips. _____
19. Today, descendants of Vikings are still observing Leif Ericson Day in the United States on October 9th. _____

Write **G** for gerund or **P** for participle above each underlined word below to indicate its form.

Exploring is in our history. By reading, we get a sense of how astonishing that exploration must have been. The exploring of North America was done by early Vikings. Perhaps we should be calling this area North Vikingland. The braving of the elements enabled the Vikings in settling hostile lands. The fear of Indian attacks is a surprising reason for the Norsemen to have left the New World. The speaking of some Scandinavian language might be standard in North America had the Vikings remained. Returning to North America 1,800 years after their first settlements, the Scandinavians have been influencing the culture ever since. The settling of cold areas such as Minnesota and the Dakotas was accomplished by Scandinavians. These descendants of Vikings are still showing the spunk of their ancient race.

**Try This!**

Write what you think is a typical Norse adventure. Using gerunds and participles when you can, include the people the adventurers might have met and the danger they might have faced on sea and land. Make it as exciting as you can.

〈23〉 FS-30047 Grammar

# Prepositions

Name _____

**Prepositions** connect ideas to each other. Below is a list of common prepositions.

| | | | | | | | | | |
|---|---|---|---|---|---|---|---|---|---|
| about | above | across | after | along | at | before | behind | beside | by |
| down | except | for | from | in | inside | into | like | near | of |
| off | on | out | outside | over | past | since | through | to | toward |
| under | underneath | until | up | upon | with | within | | | |

Some prepositions contain more than one word: *according to, aside from, in front of, instead of, across from, because of, in place of, on account of.*

A preposition relates a noun or pronoun to another word. *Eskimos live in the far North.* The preposition *in* connects *Eskimos* to *North.*

## Practice Makes Perfect

Underline the prepositions in each sentence below.

1. Eskimos are a people who live in the Arctic.
2. They live among the musk oxen and caribou.
3. In winter, Eskimos make shelters of sod or snow.
4. Most Eskimos have traditionally lived near the sea.
5. Traditional Eskimos live in shelters made from animal skins in summer.
6. They catch fish, hunt whales and seals, and live like their ancestors.
7. It takes special skills and fortitude to live with the seals and polar bears.
8. Since the 1800s, Eskimos' lifestyles have changed.
9. Some now travel by snowmobile.
10. Because of the influence of modern conveniences, their lives are often easier.
11. Instead of the word Eskimo, these people call themselves *Inuit* or *Yuit,* meaning people.
12. Snow covers most of the Eskimo country from September until June.
13. On account of living in small communities, the people must depend on each other.
14. About 100,000 Eskimos live in areas of Russia, Alaska, Canada, and Greenland.
15. Eskimos have light brown skin, straight black hair, and wide faces with high cheekbones.
16. They live in one of the coldest, harshest regions of the world.
17. They resemble both the Siberians of northern Asia and the Native Americans across the Bering Sea.
18. Most scientists classify Native Americans outside the Eskimo race.
19. In the past, the prehistoric ancestors of both the Eskimos and the Natives Americans lived in Siberia.
20. Around the Arctic Circle, hardy Eskimos live with cold, ice, and dangerous animals like the polar bear.

FS-30047 Grammar

# Prepositional Phrases—Part I

Name _____

A **prepositional phrase** is a group of words. It begins with a preposition and ends with a noun or pronoun that is the object of the preposition. The object can be compound (composed of more than one word). *Eskimos are an indigenous people of the North.* The prepositional phrase is *of the North,* and the object is the noun *North.*

*Eskimos live by their wits, strength, and courage. By their wits, strength, and courage* is the prepositional phrase, and the objects of the phrase are the nouns *wits, strength,* and *courage.*

## Practice Makes Perfect

Underline each prepositional phrase in the story below. Circle the object of the phrase.

Ice covers most of the Arctic Ocean in winter. Early Eskimos cut holes in the ice to go fishing. They would spear the fish through the water. The most common fish is the Arctic char, found in the seas. Nowadays, many Eskimos use modern equipment instead of spears. These changes have made the old way of life disappear in many areas.

Animals of the north include Arctic foxes, Arctic hares, musk oxen, Arctic wolves, polar bears, seals, and whales. Most caribou live in the Arctic only a few months of the year. They move to the south in spring and stay until fall. Since ancient times, Eskimos have been hunting this game.

Do Eskimos find plants among the icy floes and bergs? During the summer, lichens, mosses, and small shrubs grow within Eskimo territory. Instead of forests, these plants bring Eskimos a bit of green in their white-covered land.

Using the prepositional phrases below, write a story comparing and contrasting life in your town to that of the Eskimos. Underline each prepositional phrase you write. It's okay to use some that aren't on the list below. Finish your story on the back of this page.

| | | | |
|---|---|---|---|
| around our town | in the mall (or stores) | with my friends | inside my room |
| beyond the school | along the highway | within my family | in front of my house |
| among my neighbors | except for the weather | on the water | during the day |
| at night | in the winter | in place of seals and whales | |

_____

_____

_____

_____

_____

**Try This!** Write some of the advantages traditional Eskimos might have over people in other regions. What might they be able to do that you can't?

# Subordinate Clauses

Name _____

A prepositional phrase does not have a subject and a predicate. A **subordinate clause** does, and that's the main difference between the two. The two are often confused. Although the subordinate clause has both a subject and a predicate, it cannot stand alone. It is always used with an independent clause. It begins with one of the following words: **after, although, as, before, since, until, when, where,** and **while.** Since some of these words are also prepositions, it is easy to confuse prepositional phrases with subordinate clauses.

*Etiquette is a set of rules for behavior when people socialize with each other.* The subordinate clause is *when people socialize with each other.* It has a subject, *people,* and a predicate, *socialize with each other*, but cannot stand alone.

## Practice Makes Perfect

Read the sentences below about etiquette. Underline the subordinate clauses in each one.

1. People get along better when they observe rules of etiquette.

2. Follow rules of etiquette since people scorn those who don't.

3. People may be uncomfortable until they learn the etiquette of a country they're visiting.

4. Some rules may seem strange to us before we understand them.

5. Be careful not to insult someone while you are still learning the rules.

6. When we see a friend, it is polite to greet him or her.

7. After entering an elevator, men used to take off their hats in the presence of women.

8. Men haven't worn hats much since the 1950s.

9. It is polite to shake hands when you meet someone new.

10. Long ago, only men shook hands since it was not appropriate for women to do so.

11. Since there are many occasions to do so, it is important to know how to shake hands.

12. Grip the hand firmly while you resist the urge to show your strength.

13. Young children are taught manners when they are very young.

14. They learn to say *please* and *thank you* although they do forget sometimes.

15. Introduce people before there is an awkward silence.

16. Good taste is different from etiquette although the two are connected.

17. It is in bad taste to speak too loud, while it is annoying to hear someone whisper.

18. Chewing with your mouth open is rude, while making chomping noises is even worse.

19. Don't snap gum when you're with others, as you'll be considered a person without taste or manners.

20. After you watch others with taste and manners, you can learn how to behave well.

FS-30047 Grammar

# Prepositional Phrases—Part II

Name _____

When you use both prepositional phrases and subordinate clauses, you add interest and variety to your writing. Prepositional phrases can be either **adverb phrases** or **adjective phrases**. *We have gone to dinner at the Davis house often. At the Davis house* is an adverb phrase as it tells **where** we have gone. *The Davises are classy people with great manners. With great manners* is an adjective phrase as it tells **what kind of** manners the Davises have.

## Practice Makes Perfect

Read the sentences below. Underline the prepositional phrases. Circle the subordinate clauses. After each sentence that contains a prepositional phrase, write **A** for an adverb phrase and **Adj.** for an adjective phrase on the lines. (Hint: Remember that subordinate clauses begin with words like *after, although, as, before, since, until, when, where,* and *while.*)

1. I went to my new friend's house last night. _____

2. I really wanted to make a good impression on her family. _____

3. When the soup came, I didn't slurp it up. _____

4. I didn't even drink from the finger bowl. _____

5. Instead, I dipped my napkin in the bowl. _____

6. Since people were looking at me, I knew I was correct. _____

7. I delicately wiped the napkin on my face and cleaned my ears. _____

8. I know that one should not sit at the table dirty. _____

9. While everyone was eating, I made polite conversation. _____

10. I told them about the dead mouse my cat had brought home. _____

11. At that time, people began to cough. _____

12. I guess colds are going around town. _____

13. I hope I didn't catch anything from those people. _____

14. I was very hungry, and I said, "Hey you behind the salt, please pass it." _____

15. My friend's mother fell into a faint. _____

16. I remember that this happened after the dessert. _____

17. I dug into that dessert with a vengeance. _____ _____

18. I was sorry it had nuts because I had to spit them onto the plate. _____

19. I must say I enjoy entertainment during a meal. _____

20. When my pet frog came out from underneath my shirt, it was very funny. _____

21. I'm sure I'll be invited to her house again soon. _____

**Try This!** Write a list of new rules for etiquette that you think people should use. Make them funny, silly, or outrageous.

# Essential Clauses

Name _____

A complex sentence contains an **independent clause** and a **subordinate clause**. The independent clause can stand alone, and it expresses a complete thought. The subordinate clause cannot stand alone and does not express a complete thought. Sometimes the subordinate clause is an adjective clause. It describes a noun or pronoun in the independent clause. It may begin with one of the following relative pronouns: **who, whom, whose, which,** or **that**. *We study the people who believed in many gods. Who believed in many gods* is the adjective clause. It is an **essential clause** that makes the meaning of the sentence clear. It does not require a comma. This sentence clarifies something about the vague "people." So an essential clause is an adjective clause that makes the meaning of a sentence clear.

## Practice Makes Perfect

Underline each essential clause in the sentences below. Write what it makes clear and why it is essential.

1. We read the words of the writer who wrote about the most important beliefs of the Greeks.

   _____

2. The Greeks developed many ideas that we still live by today.

   _____

3. The Greeks formulated ideas that tell us right from wrong.

   _____

4. The Greeks believed in gods whose wrath they greatly feared.

   _____

5. Greek teachers had students who learned about their culture and its place in the world.

   _____

6. Scholars went to classes that were often taught by a philosopher.

   _____

7. Acting in and writing comic and tragic plays are among the things that Greeks did first.

   _____

8. The Greeks devised some rules that today govern our ideas of politics, rights, and duties.

   _____

9. The Greeks developed a democracy whose ideals we still respect today.

   _____

10. Archaeologists have unearthed Greek artifacts that tell us exactly how the Greeks lived.

    _____

11. They have found amphorae that prove that the Greeks traded products such as olive oil.

    _____

12. Amphorae are jars that the Greeks used as containers for a variety of things.

    _____

# Nonessential Clauses

Some adjective clauses in complex sentences are **nonessential clauses**. This means that the sentences can stand alone without those clauses, and they aren't needed to make the sentences more clear. The nonessential clause gives more information, but that information is not needed for the sentence to make sense. Commas set the nonessential clause apart from the rest of the sentence. It is an adjective clause. *Athens, which was one of many city-states, was the seat of democracy.* The nonessential clause in this complex sentence is *which was one of many city-states.* The rest of the sentence can stand without it.

## Practice Makes Perfect

Underline the nonessential clause in each sentence below.

1. Sparta, which became a Greek military state, was ruled by a small group of men.

2. The Greeks, who were blessed with a mild climate, did much work and play outdoors.

3. The Spartans, who loved war, were defeated by the Persians at the battle of Thermopylae.

4. Sparta's large population, which was constantly growing, made the Spartans stretch out toward the lands of other people.

5. Greek slaves, who were captured by the Spartans, were called helots.

6. These slaves, who outnumbered the Spartans, farmed the soil and gave most of their produce to their master.

7. Spartan boys, who were examined for good health at birth, were trained to be soldiers at the age of seven.

8. Babies who were thin, frail, or sick, no matter how their parents felt about it, were thrown into a deep hole to die.

9. The Spartan culture, which seems cruel to us, had no tolerance for those who were not strong in body.

10. The young boys, who slept on hard beds and wore few clothes, were trained to withstand the greatest hardships.

11. Spartan girls, although they were not trained to be soldiers, were also expected to have strong, healthy bodies.

12. This warrior people, who were so proud of physical strength, cared very little about improving their minds and learning new ideas.

13. After a few years, when they became teenagers, young men would be sent to the woods without food or water.

14. The future soldier, who would have to steal or find food, would starve if he couldn't fend for himself.

15. These young men, who had to serve in the army until age 60, spent more time with their fellow soldiers than with their families.

**Try This!** How would you feel about being a Spartan boy? What would you do if you were left in the woods with neither food nor drink?

**Page 2**
1. declarative   2. declarative
3. interrogative   4. imperative
5. exclamatory   6. declarative
7. interrogative   8. imperative
9. exclamatory   10. declarative
11. declarative   12. interrogative
13. declarative   14. imperative
15. declarative   16. declarative
17. exclamatory   18. declarative
19. imperative   20. interrogative
21. exclamatory   22. declarative
23. declarative

**Page 3**
1. People didn't know their lives were changing.
2. They could scare off many wild animals with fire.
3. Keeping the fire going was a great responsibility.
4. Soon humans learned how to make tools and weapons.
5. A man with a stone would hit the stone with a stick.
6. A piece of stone would break off. It would be sharp.
7. This sharp tool could be used for cutting, slicing, and skinning.
8. Each member of the tribe had a job.
9. There were hunters, gatherers, toolmakers, firekeepers, and cooks.
10. Just as we do today, humans have always tried to make their lives better.
they, them, they, they, they, see, they, you, know, Look, like, they

**Page 4**
Animals, movies, movie, century, Animals, dogs, horses, heroes, villains, films, Rin Tin Tin, hero, German shepherd, guys, Lassie, movies, fans, Lassies, dog, Horses, place, movies, Cowboys, Lone Ranger, Roy Rogers, horses, Silver, Trigger, Silver, horse, Trigger, palomino, animals, parts, rats, frogs, dolphins, snakes, bears, wolves, rabbits, ferrets, actors, animals
1. Owners, pride, actor
2. Animals, love, trainers
3. groups, presence, movie sets
4. animals, respect
5. Cruelty, animals
6. Love, animals, people, movies
7. dogs   8. awards
9. animals   10. horses
11. Trainers

**Page 5**
1. team   2. pride
3. gaggle   4. pack
5. flock
6. She starred in many movies and television series.
7. It was the sad story of a brave, loyal dog.
8. He was a huge St. Bernard.
9. They loved the movie "101 Dalmatians."
10. She is one of the most famous animal stars ever.
11. They earn a lot of money.
12. me, I   13. them, D
14. him, D   15. us, I
16. them, I

**Page 6**
1. take   2. bring
3. bring   4. Bring
5. take   6. brought
7. teach   8. teach
9. learn   10. taught
11. learned   12. lie
13. lay   14. lay
15. laid

**Page 7**
1. left   2. let
3. left   4. leave
5. left   6. leave
7. let   8. leave
9. Leave   10. left
6.-8. Answers will vary.
Sit, sit, set, set, sat, set, set, sat, set

**Page 8**
1. *Oliver Twist* was written by Charles Dickens. Oliver seemed to be a poor orphan.
2. *Dombey and Son* by Dickens is a favorite story of my cousin. Dickens wrote it to stress the evils of loving money.
3. *Little Lord Fauntleroy* was written by Frances Hodgson Burnett. Fauntleroy had a rich old uncle.
4. Lucy Boston wrote stories about the children of Green Knowe. The children were ghostly.
5. Heidi is a girl who lives with her grandfather and some goats in the Swiss Alps. She and her grandfather find each other strange at first.
6. Stories about Harriet the Spy and her friends are much appreciated by the kids in our class. The kids enjoy adventures.
7. *The Great Brain* books were written by John Fitzgerald for boys and girls. The books are really fun.
8. Anastasia Krupnik is a heroine created by Lois Lowry. Anastasia Krupnik is smart, brave, and funny.

**Page 9**
1. boys, They
2. boy or Jim Hawkins, He
3. series, It
4. Tom Sawyer, He
5. Antoine St.-Exupéry, He
6. Huckleberry Finn, He
7. four sisters, They
8. book, It
9. Adventures, They
10. *Aladdin* or *Ali Baba and the Forty Thieves*, They
tales, They, Paul Bunyan, He, Babe, It, Paul Bunyan, He, Paul, He, Pecos Bill, He, Mike Fink, who, John Henry, who, John Chapman, He, Johnny Appleseed, He, he

**Page 10**
1. farmed, learned, plant
2. discovered, domesticate
3. created
4. plowed
5. helped build
6. worked, build
7. rank
8. overflowed
9. waited, water
10. dug, direct
11. paid
12. bartered
13. sell, help
14. depended
15. shared
16. P   17. P
18. P   19. P
20. P   21. M
22. P   23. P
24. M

**Page 11**
1. was, N   2. grew, A
3. was, A   4. are, N
5. was, A   6. were, A
7. were, A   8. is, A
9. were, N   10. were, A
11. were, N   12. were, N
13. were, A   14. is, N
15. flooded (intransitive verb)
16. flooded, fields (direct object)
17. fought, water (direct object)
18. fought (intransitive verb)

# Answers

**Page 12**
1. Thomas Edison invented the light bulb.
2. Da Vinci thought man could fly.
3. Someone will invent a ship that will take us to Mars.
4. The computer revolutionized the business world.
5. Many inventions changed the world in the nineteenth century.
6. Orville and Wilbur Wright worked on an invention called the airplane.
7. Samuel Morse has a code that he invented named after him.
8. The wheel was the greatest invention the world has known.
9. Television is seen by hundreds of millions of people.
10. Simple inventions such as gloves and zippers changed the world, too.

are (will be), have invented (will invent), will invent (invent), imagine (imagined), fly (flew), zoom (zoomed), makes (made)

**Page 13**
1. have existed
2. have marveled, have visited
3. have seen
4. have experienced
5. have swayed
6. have intrigued
7. has absorbed
8. has housed
9. have caused, has creaked
10. have thrilled
11. had challenged
12. had thought
13. had waited
14. had run
15. had happened
16. had seen
17. had kept
18. had come

**Page 14**
What do the star-nosed mole, people, and the gigantic blue whale have in common? If you said they are all mammals, you are right. They all breathe air through their lungs and nurse their young. They have a more well-developed brain and hair. If you said they all also maintain a constant body temperature, you are right! All mammals, except for a few, for example the echidna and platypus (both of them are from Australia) are born live. They lay eggs. There are about 4,000 kinds of mammals on Earth.

**Page 15**
1. CS    2. CS
3. SS    4. CS
5. SS    6. SS
7. CS    8. CS
9. CS    10. CS
11. The sloth seems lazy and weak, but it has powerful claws for defense.
12. The sloth must stay in trees for long periods because it can be easy prey on the ground.
13. Sloths eat leaves, buds, and young twigs, and they sleep during the day.

**Page 16**
seriously, really, humongously, quietly, away, just, awhile, dejectedly, wonderfully, beautifully, cavernously, quickly, last, loudly, safely, so, well, ever, really, grouchily, laughingly, usually, all, hardly, obnoxiously
1. gnarly (how), sometimes (when)
2. Maybe (when), scarily (how)
3. hard (how)
4. Perhaps (when), easily (how)
5. dangerously (how), together (how)
6. Maybe (when), finally (when), slightly (how)
7. Later (when)
8. hardly (how much), ever (when)
9. once (when)
10. definitely (how)

**Page 17**
1. highly, adjective
2. almost, adjective
3. totally, adjective
4. really, adverb
5. almost, adverb
6. quite, adverb
7. terribly, adverb
8. completely, adjective
9. totally, adjective
10. excitingly, adjective
11. more
12. less
13. funniest
14. better/more

**Page 18**
1. every        2. Chinese
3. foreign      4. historical
5. second       6. German
7. useful       8. common
9. English      10. Native
11. larger      12. astonishing
13. educated, extensive
14. colorful    15. compound
16. mighty      17. permanent

**Page 19**
1. This, here
2. that, there
3. This
4. these, here
5. These, here
6. those
7. Those
8. that
9. Those, this, here
10. That, there
11. easier
12. better, younger
13. harder
14. better

**Page 20**
been, dirtying, proven, been, polluting, throwing, compared, poisoning, using, helped, resulting, burning, spilling, been, going
1. garbage, trash
2. People, Earth
3. Earth        4. laws, pollution
5. representatives
6. people
7. we           8. cars
9. cars         10. pollutants
11. illness     12. monuments
13. Earth       14. planet
15. Earth

**Page 21**
Answers will vary.
1. By treating sewage plants, we can make the water cleaner.
2. Settling in the lungs, smog can make us sick with asthma or other illnesses.
3. By failing to save Earth, we will make our planet unlivable.
4. By recycling cans, bottles, and newspapers, we can make Earth cleaner.
5. Driving cars that use lots of gas will cause us to increase pollution.
6. We can use containers for pickup and collect recyclables for money.
7. Earning money for a field trip enabled us to go to science camp.
8. Finding garbage in the street, we picked it up and threw it in the proper place.
9. Realizing the danger of pollution, we all read the article in the paper.
10. Being a person who cares about the environment, I wrote an article that was carried by the newspaper.
11-15. Answers will vary.

## Page 22
1. Leading, SS
2. outlawing, DO
3. planning, DO
4. Being, SS
5. Being, SS
6. exploring, DO
7. Adventuring, SS
8. forbidding, DO
9. farming, DO, raising, DO
10. falling, DO
11. Exploring, SS
12. Telling, SS
13. growing, DO
14. Sailing, SS
15. seeking, DO

## Page 23
1. exploring, gerund
2. preaching, verb phrase
3. sailing, verb phrase
4. sailing, adjective, growing, gerund
5. making, verb phrase
6. thinking, verb phrase
7. building, gerund
8. logging, adjective
9. Building, verb phrase
10. returning, verb phrase
11. drowning, adjective
12. giving, verb phrase
13. Discovering, gerund
14. Sailing, gerund
15. living, verb phrase
16. returning, adjective
17. continuing, verb phrase
18. attacking, adjective
19. observing, verb phrase

gerund, participle, participle, gerund, participle, gerund, participle, participle, gerund, participle, participle, gerund, participle

## Page 24
1. in
2. among
3. In, of
4. near
5. in, from, in
6. like
7. with
8. Since
9. by
10. Because of, of
11. Instead of
12. of, from, until
13. On account of, in, on
14. About, in, of
15. with
16. in, of, of
17. of, across
18. outside
19. In, of, in
20. Around, with, like

## Page 25
of the **Arctic Ocean**, in **winter**, in the **ice**, to go **fishing**, through the **water**, in the **seas**, instead of **spears**, of **life**, in many **areas**, of the **north**, in the **Arctic**, of the **year**, to the **south**, in **spring**, until **fall**, Since ancient **times**, among the icy **floes** and **bergs**, During the **summer**, within Eskimo **territory**, Instead of **forests**, of **green**, in their white-covered **land**
Stories will vary.

## Page 26
1. when they observe rules of etiquette
2. since people scorn those who don't
3. until they learn the etiquette of a country they're visiting
4. before we understand them
5. while you are still learning the rules
6. When we see a friend
7. After entering an elevator
8. since the 1950s
9. when you meet someone new
10. since it was not appropriate for women to do so
11. Since there are many occasions to do so
12. while you resist the urge to show your strength
13. when they are very young
14. although they do forget sometimes
15. before there is an awkward silence
16. although the two are connected
17. while it is annoying to hear someone whisper
18. while making chomping noises is even worse
19. as you'll be considered a person without taste or manners
20. After you watch others with taste and manners

## Page 27
1. to my new friend's house, PP (A)
2. on her family, PP (A)
3. When the soup came, SC
4. from the finger bowl, PP (A)
5. in the bowl, PP (A)
6. Since people were looking at me, SC
7. on my face, PP (A)
8. at the table, PP (A)
9. While everyone was eating, SC
10. about the dead mouse, PP (Adj.)
11. At that time, SC
12. around town, PP (A)
13. from those people, PP (A)
14. behind the salt, PP (A)
15. into a faint, PP (A)
16. after the dessert, PP(A)
17. into that dessert, PP (A), with a vengeance, PP (Adj.)
18. onto the plate, PP (A)
19. during a meal, PP (A)
20. When my pet frog came out from underneath my shirt, SC
21. to her house, PP (A)

## Page 28
1. who wrote about the most important beliefs of the Greeks, Tells what the writer wrote about
2. that we still live by today, Tells about our relationships to the ideas
3. that tell us right from wrong, Tells what kind of ideas
4. whose wrath they greatly feared, Tells something about their beliefs in their gods
5. who learned about their culture and its place in the world, Tells what students learned
6. that were often taught by a philosopher, Tells who taught them
7. that Greeks did first, Tells two of the things they did first
8. that today govern our ideas of politics, rights, and duties, Tells how the rules they devised are used today
9. whose ideals we still respect today, Tells how we regard their democratic ideals
10. that tell us exactly how the Greeks lived, Tells what information was provided by the artifacts
11. that prove that the Greeks traded products such as olive oil, Tells what was found out from the amphorae
12. that the Greeks used as containers for a variety of things, Tells the use of amphorae

## Page 29
1. which became a Greek military state
2. who were blessed with a mild climate
3. who loved war
4. which was constantly growing
5. who were captured by the Spartans
6. who outnumbered the Spartans
7. who were examined for good health at birth
8. no matter how their parents felt about it
9. which seems cruel to us
10. who slept on hard beds and wore few clothes
11. although they were not trained to be soldiers
12. who were so proud of physical strength
13. when they became teenagers
14. who would have to steal or find food
15. who had to serve in the army until age 60